The New VEGAN SOAP Cookbook

How to Make Homemade Plant Based Soap

By: Zakia Ringgold

The New Vegan Soap Cookbook - How to Make Homemade Plant Based Soap

By: Zakia Ringgold

All rights reserved. No part of this book may be reproduced in whole or in part in any form by any means without the express written consent of the author. Requests for permission to reproduce portions of this book should be addressed to **zakia@livesoapschool.com**.

Limits of Liability and Disclaimer of Warranty: This book is strictly for informational and educational purposes. The author and/or publisher shall have neither liability nor responsibility for errors, omissions or for any loss or damage claimed to be related to the information contained in this book.
Copyright © 2018 Zakia Ringgold
All rights reserved.

ISBN: 9781728898971

Dedication

This book is dedicated to my mom for her unconditional love, support and constant encouragement. What she poured into me is a reflection of all that I am and aspire to be in this lifetime.

Thanks Mom

II. Why I wrote this book

My product line started out incorporating both animal and plant based oils and butters. I wondered, "could I make a 100% vegan soap that had all of the qualities of my initial creations". In an effort to get as natural as possible, I set out on a journey to formulate an all vegetable based soap and to my surprise these creations turned into my best sellers.

As I looked on the market for vegan specific resources the options were limited, readers of my first books "The New Soap Makers Cookbooks" series and followers of the Live Soap School community wanted more information on plant based recipes. Hence The Vegan Soap Cookbook was created with my experimentation and those results are now in your hands. I hope you find inspiration to either convert your products to all plant based or extend what you are currently making to include vegan only options.

This book is written in a no-fluff manner. There are no fancy, hard to acquire ingredients or extraneous techniques. This is done intentionally to ensure you get the necessary foundation to understand the soap making process and more importantly to see the beauty in simplicity.

Bubbles and Hugs

-*SoapLadyZ*

III. How to use this book

This book is divided into 4 sections: an introduction, recipes ingredient profiles and next steps. Feel free to read from beginning to end or jump directly to a section that interests you most.

Introduction
The introduction makes the case for vegan soap, supplies needed to get started, and seven simple steps to make soap using the cold process method. Start here if you are brand new to making soap or if you just want a review of the basic process.

Recipes
The recipes section shares my favorite time-tested, fool proof plant based recipes, with easy to acquire ingredients. Jump to this section if you are ready to start experimenting with vegan only ingredients.

Ingredients
If you are ready to start creating your own recipes, the ingredients section is where you should begin . This section highlights 20 of the most popular soap making ingredients along with their qualities, characteristics and usage rates.

QR Codes
You will notice various QR codes throughout the book. These will take you to additional resources and bonus videos at **LiveSoapSchool.com**.

I have created these to supplement some areas that may need

additional explanation or hands-on demonstration. To access the resources from the QR code, use your smart phone camera to scan the QR code and be taken to the online resource.

This book is meant to be a primer for your entry into making plant based soap. The most important thing you can do after reading this book is to make your own soap using the tried and true recipes or by formulating your own.

One final note about recipes, with any and all recipes you create or find online or in any book (including this one) you should always run the calculations through a soap calculator. If you need help with using a soap calculator or formulating your recipes, head over to **class.LiveSoapSchool.com** and enroll in our soap making classes or request a recipe formulation session.

Table Of Contents

1.0 Why Go Vegan 1

1.1 Supplies You Need to Make Soap From Scratch.....4

1.2 Ingredients Make the Maker 6

1.3 Working Safely with Lye aka Sodium Hydroxide 8

1.4 Steps to Make Cold Process Soap 10

1.5 Using Milk Alternatives in Soap Making 16

Part 2 - Recipes 18

    2.1 Simple Soap 19

    2.2 Baby Soap 19

    2.3 Bastille Soap Recipe 20

    2.4 Calming Conditioning Bar 20

    2.5 Healing Wonder Recipe 21

    2.6 Lemongrass 21

    2.7 Avocado Soap 22

    2.8 Cucumber Pore Perfection 23

    2.9 Egyptian Milk Soap 24

    2.10 Dead Sea Facial Bar 25

    2.11 Soothing Skin Soap 26

    2.12 Cooling Cucumber and Aloe Vera Soap 27

    2.13 One Oil Wonder 28

    2.14 Palm Free Recipe 28

    2.15 Activated Charcoal Cleansing Bar 29

    2.16 Sea Salt Bar 30

Part 3 - Creating your own Vegan Soap Recipes 31

3.0 The DNA of Oils and Butters 32

3.1 Saponification, SAP value and SuperFat 39

3.2 Vegan Ingredient Profiles 41

    3.3 Almond Oil 42

    3.4 Avocado Oil 43

    3.5 Babassu Oil 43

    3.6 Canola Oil 44

    3.7 Castor Oil 44

    3.8 Cocoa Butter 45

    3.9 Coconut Oil 45

    3.10 Grapeseed Oil 46

    3.11 Jojoba Oil 46

    3.12 Kokum Butter 47

    3.13 Mango Butter 47

    3.14 Neem Oil 48

    3.15 Olive Oil 48

    3.16 Palm Oil 49

    3.17 Palm Kernel Oil 49

    3.18 Rice Bran Oil 50

    3.19 Sesame Seed Oil 50

    3.20 Shea Butter 51

    3.21 Sunflower Oil 51

4.0 A Makers Tale 53

4.1 Stay Connected 55

4.2 Read My Books for Soap Makers 57

4.3 About the Author 58

1.0 Why Go Vegan

The simplest answer to the question of why go vegan is, it's what nature intended. If you are making natural products it is best to utilize the most natural ingredients you can find both for practicality and the benefits they offer the skin and our environment. Deciding to make natural soap with plant based ingredients is actually quite easy once you are able to identify the qualities they lend to your final product. In most cases there is a vegan alternative to any and all animal based ingredients.

Many people choose to make their own natural soap to control the ingredients in their families skincare. By choosing plant-based ingredients for your soap creations you are selecting ingredients for their known benefits. Not only will you control ingredients you are also creating a sustainable product. This is a win-win for your family and the environment.

If you sell handmade bath and body products you will notice that the market is now demanding more eco-friendly skincare. Increasingly consumers are becoming more conscientious about what they are putting in their bodies and ON their bodies. Don't you want to offer them the best ingredients? This is not to say that the animal counter-parts to plant based ingredients are inferior but in my experience there is no soap I couldn't make using all vegetable ingredients. Plant based ingredients offer a wealth of benefits to the skin including: cleansing, conditioning, moisturizing and nourishing. All of which are highly sought after with handmade soap.

There is an old proverb that states "give a man a fish, feed him for a day. Teach a man to fish and feed him for a lifetime". My goal with this cookbook is to teach you how to fish. While this cookbook offers several of my personal soap recipes, it is even more important for you to understand "WHY" particular ingredients are selected and incorporated into soap recipes.

This will allow you to create your own recipes if you choose to do so. More over it will also allow you to speak confidently about your soap along with the qualities it offers the skin. This cookbook also includes Vegan Soap Profiles of the top plant-based oils and butters used in soap making. These profiles can serve you as a quick reference for each oil's SAP values, fatty acid profile, recommended usage rates and skin qualities.

In the upcoming chapters you will gain all the knowledge you need to:
- Follow simple instructions and recipes to make your own Vegan Soap from scratch
- Select ingredients based on the qualities you want in your soap
- Understand how fatty acids and SAP values impact soap recipes

Most importantly use your imagination, have fun, experiment and remember the only failed batch of soap is the one you didn't make.

Before going any further, take a moment to reflect on and write about what you wish to accomplish by reading this book.

The simple act of writing takes it from just wishing and thinking about it to creating in the physical form. Make a promise to yourself that you won't just read it but you will actually put something specific into action.

1.1 Supplies You Need to Make Soap From Scratch

Many of the supplies you will need to get started making soap can be found right in your kitchen or garage. There is one rule that you must adhere to: ***"if you use equipment for soap, it can only be used for soap making going forward".*** I wouldn't want you to have the taste of soap in your family's favorite meal. So please adhere to this rule. If you need to buy your supplies start at local garage sales, second hand stores, consignment shops, thrift shops or discount stores. If all else fails there is an abundance of online sites where you can find what you need.

You do not need the most expensive gadgets and gizmos to get started. Save your money for the ingredients. If you absolutely must go online to shop, I have created a shopping list as a starting point but you can do your own research to find bargains.

You can access the shopping list with links at: **livesoapschool.com/ suppliestomakesoap**

Supplies Needed:
- Reliable Kitchen Scale that measures in grams and ounces
- Heat resistant mixing bowls to measure and melt your oils
- Glass Measuring cup
- Candy Thermometer or Infrared Thermometer
- Heat Resistant plastic or stainless steel pitcher to create your lye solution
- 3 to 4 silicone spatulas for stirring and scrapping your bowls
- Plastic Mixing Bowls
- Mold to set your cold process soap (plastic, wooden or silicone)
- Stick Blender to mix lye and oils
- Stainless Steel Pot

You can go cheap/used on most supplies but you must look for quality in the tools you will use repeatedly. Get a quality stick blender as this is the magic wand in the soap making process and you will be happy you invested here.

As for your choice of molds. Virtually anything can be used as a soap mold. You can use old drawers, yogurt containers, plastic storage bins, and even old milk cartons. If you don't have a lot of money to get started, consider up-cycling things around the house. You will need to line them with freezer paper or plastic bags to assist with releasing the hardened soap but you can get really creative with your choice of molds.

Many online suppliers have a wealth of wooden, plastic and silicone molds. I have not had much success with plastic molds and prefer to work with wooden or silicone molds. The molds I use are specially crafted for making soap and you can find them priced from basic and inexpensive to custom crafted and very expensive. If you are prepared to buy a professional soap mold do some research, read the reviews and comparison shop.

1.2 Ingredients Make the Maker

One of the critical components of your soap is the actual ingredients you select and use in your recipes. When we discuss ingredients this includes: lye, oils, butter, scents, additives and colorants. Each one will make an impact on the outcome of the final batch and each one can make or break an entire recipe.

As hand crafted soap making gains in popularity more exotic ingredients are introduced on the market. This is where you will need to exercise a little discernment or you run the risk of stockpiling 20 different ingredients that offer the same qualities to your creations. Many of these ingredients will expire before they can be used or fail to live up to the hype. Not every oil is created equal and this is also true for suppliers as well.

Remember what you put in the soap pot literally comes out in the wash, if you skimp on quality ingredients it will show in your final bars. Listed below are the basic staple ingredients every soap maker should have in their soap room.

- Sodium Hydroxide
- Distilled Water
- Olive Oil
- Castor Oil
- Coconut Oil
- Shea Butter
- Cocoa Butter
- Palm Oil
- Approved Soap Colorant
- Essential oils or Fragrance oils of your choice

There is no magic bullet for finding the perfect color or scent. Soap making is scientific and there is always a bit of chemistry at work. Color and scent is where much of your trial and error will come into play. Whenever you are trying a new ingredient, start small. Many suppliers offer discounts based on the quantity of what is ordered. What good is it to save money if you hate the ingredient?

It's perfectly fine to buy base ingredients like lye, oils and butters in bulk, but you must remember that EVERYTHING has a shelf life and an expiration date. It's not saving you any money if you end up wasting the ingredient because it expires before you can use it. A general rule of thumb is, if you can't use it within 3 months…don't buy it.

When I first started making soap I would stockpile ingredients because I knew "at some point" I would use it. I just wanted to have it on hand "just in case". Needless to say, my "some point" never came to fruition and I had to toss the expired ingredients. If you want to start wasting money, start stockpiling ingredients and watch those expirations dates creep up ever so quickly. If you don't have an immediate need, don't buy it.

You can find a list of reputable Soap Suppliers at:
LiveSoapSchool.com/recommended-suppliers

1.3 Working Safely with Lye aka Sodium Hydroxide

If I had a dollar for each time someone asked "Can Soap be made without lye?" I would easily be a millionaire. There is not a live stream or local soap making class I have completed where this question doesn't invariably appear. Luckily I've been live streaming for a while and many of my regular viewers are able to answer the question before I even see it. If you are reading this book you may not have seen a live stream so I will explain further.

Sodium Hydroxide (NAOH) is used to make hard bar soap. Potassium Hydroxide (KOH) is used to make liquid soap. Both Sodium Hydroxide and Potassium Hydroxide are commonly referred to as lye. Lye is required to create the chemical reaction known as Saponification. If you don't use lye, you don't get soap. Have you ever tried to mix oils and water? It just doesn't work. The only exception to this rule is with melt and pour glycerin soap where the manufacturer has already completed the saponification process with the lye for you.

Soap is made by combining oils and fats with a lye solution. This forces the chemical reaction known as Saponification. As long as the recipe is formulated appropriately, there will be no lye in the final batch of soap.
The trick is for you to exercise proper safety precautions when using Lye. ALL THE TIME!

Working Safely with Lye
Lye is a very caustic and corrosive substance in its raw state. You must be careful and protected when working with it. As long as you follow basic soap safety measures, you will be fine working with lye.

WHAT DOES IT MEAN TO BE SAFE WITH LYE?

Always wear gloves and goggles when working with lye and raw soap batter.
- Gloves protect your hands in the event of splashes
- Safety goggles protect your eyes

If you get lye or raw soap batter on your skin, DO NOT PANIC. Rinse the area with cold water. It can be extremely dangerous if you splash lye in your eye as it can lead to blindness. I'm not saying this to scare you I'm saying this because it's true and to remind you to ALWAYS wear goggles. You should also wear long sleeve shirts, pants and closed toe shoes as protection for your skin.

The next time someone asks you can soap be made without lye, you can confidently respond NO. The question that usually follows is "will lye be in the soap once it's ready"? Once again you can confidently answer no...if you: used proper recipe measurements, followed the soap making process and allowed for appropriate cure time. There will be no lye left in the final batch of soap.

You can watch a step by step safety demo at:
LiveSoapSchool.com/ingredients-to-success-resources

1.4 Steps to Make Cold Process Soap

With a recipe in hand and safety gear on, you can make soap in seven simple steps. Each step is important and will build upon the previous completed action. You must remember that you are working with a caustic solution and therefore you must be careful. This caution begins with your safety gear. ALWAYS wear goggles and gloves with no exception throughout all the steps.

Precision is critical when making soap and therefore you should always measure your lye, distilled water, oils and butters by weight. Never measure these ingredients by markings on a measuring cup as they are not reliable or consistent. You can use measuring spoons for additives and colorants as these measurements are typically given in teaspoons and tablespoons.

Before getting started lay out all of your supplies and ingredients so that you can work without needing to stop and look for anything. Now let's take a look at the seven steps to make soap using the cold process method.

1. **Measure and Mix the Lye Solution**
   Using a kitchen scale, measure the sodium hydroxide and distilled water in separate containers.
   Pour the sodium hydroxide into the distilled water and mix with a spatula until the solution becomes clear. The temperature of this will rise to over 180 degrees Fahrenheit so be careful not to spill or allow it to splash on your skin.

   Tip: By mixing your lye solution first, this gives you time to complete all other preparation steps while allowing the solution to cool down to a workable temperature below 100 degrees Fahrenheit.

Remember to only pour the lye into the water NOT the other way around. Also, you should never use aluminum, cast iron or tin for measuring your lye or creating a lye solution. Always use heavy duty plastic, or stainless steel.

2. **Measure and Melt the Oils and Butters**
   Using a kitchen scale, measure each oil and butter in a plastic mixing bowl. As you are first getting started you may find it easier to measure each oil and butter in a separate container. If you over pour a particular oil you can easily pour it back into it's original container without cross contaminating your other oils. Once you get comfortable pouring you can condense your measuring stage into a single container to avoid extra cleanup.

   Once all oils and butters are measured, combine into a single container and place them over a low flame to melt. You can also melt slowly in the microwave on 60 second increments. Be careful not to scorch the oils as you could lose some of the qualities. Once all melted, set aside and move on to the next step.

3. **Prepare your Mold, Fragrances, Colors and/or Additives**
   While allowing your oils and lye solution to cool down you should prepare all other ingredients for use during the soap making process. This is when you should line your mold, measure out your fragrance/essential oils, colorants and/or additives. Always measure essential oils in glass containers and avoid plastics.

   The one rule of thumb is to ensure everything is prepared BEFORE you begin mixing any lye solution with your oils and butters. This will ensure that if your soap mixture begins to move quickly you aren't slowed down by any miscellaneous searching or measuring while soaping.

4. **Mix the Lye Solution and Oils**
   Once the temperature of your lye solution and oils reaches below 110 degrees Fahrenheit, slowly pour the Lye solution into the oils. Give it a good stir with a spatula for a moment to begin the saponification process. After a minute, switch to your stick blender and pulse on low until the oils and lye solution are completely emulsified.

   Pro Tip: You will know it's completely emulsified when the oils and water no longer separate. The longer you pulse the stick blender, the thicker the mixture will become this is also known as trace.

5. **OPTIONAL - Incorporate the Color, Fragrance and Additives**
   If you are going to add any additional colorant, fragrance or additives like clays, oats or poppy seeds, now is the time. I typically prefer to add additives first, followed by colorant and fragrance last. This is also the point where your soap can start to misbehave, so it's best to add the fragrance last so you can quickly move to the next step in the soap making process. If you are using multiple colors, you will need separate containers to portion off your soap mixture into each container so each color will maintain it's integrity before pouring it into the mold.

6. **Pour the Soap into the Mold and allow it to set for 24 hours**
   Slowly pour the soap batter into your mold avoiding any splashing. By pouring slowly you minimize the creation of air bubbles and are able to get a more uniform pour. Once all of your soap batter is poured into the mold you can lightly tap it with a plastic covered mallet or by tapping the mold on your counter. This will help to pop any air bubbles that formed during the pour.

Many soap makers will spray the top of their soap with rubbing alcohol to prevent the formation of a white powdery substance which is also known as soda ash. You can also cover your mold with plastic to create a barrier between your soap and the air preventing any moisture from attaching to the top of your soap. Finally you can cover your soap to help with the saponification process and to allow it to go through what is known as the "Gel Phase". All of the steps mentioned in this paragraph are completely optional and a matter of preference.

Once you pour the soap into the mold you can simply allow it to set up for 24 hours *untouched.*

7. **Cut and Cure the Soap**
Once your soap has had a minimum of 24 hours to setup and it feels firm you can take it out of the mold. Due to the formulation of some recipes containing a higher percentage of soft oils, you may need to wait an additional 48 hours to unmold it as it may not be firm enough.

When the soap is firm, cut it into 1-2 inch bars using a sharp knife. Place the bars in a well-ventilated area out of direct sunlight and allow it to cure. During the curing process the soap will get even harder as the excess water evaporates from the bar. This is where the observing and weighing begins.

Take one of your bars and weigh it and note it's weight. Each week weigh the same bar and notate it. Once it stops losing weight or the weight remains constant for 7 days, it is fully cured and ready to use.

Most cold processed soap will complete the curing process in 4-7 weeks from the time it is cut. I know it can be very tempting to use your soap as soon as you take it out of the mold but you must allow it to cure so that it is mild and can last as long as possible. Just like fine wine, cold processed soap only gets better with time.

You can watch me go through the entire process here: livesoapschool.com/coldprocesssoap

SOAPERS NOTES:

Based on the information you just read, use this page to take notes on what you have on hand and what you will need to buy to make soap.

1.5 Using Milk Alternatives in Soap Making

Many recipes will often call for Goats milk or Buttermilk but did you know there is a plant based alternative for these ingredients? You can substitute the animal milk with either coconut milk, soy milk or almond milk to get a similar outcome and qualities in your soap. The one condition with using milk in any recipe is that the natural sugar in milk tends to caramelize which can result in brown colored soap and therefore most be treated accordingly to minimize this effect.

To use milk in your recipes, you can substitute all or a percentage of the water portion of your recipe with milk. You read that right, any soap recipe can be converted to a milk recipe by using milk as the water content.

But how do we make the substitution? Since you will be using the milk content to make your lye solution, you must freeze the milk before using it mixing with the lye. Otherwise you will have burnt milk and/or a browning of your soap. Therefore you must prep the milk at least one day in advance by measuring and freezing it.

Once the soap is poured into the mold, you would also place it in a refrigerator or freezer to prevent the soap from continuing to heat up in the Gel phase. One thing that should be evident with all of this is the attention to temperature.
- You want to ensure the milk is frozen to prevent caramelizing when mixing with the lye
- Your oils need to be hot enough to prevent a false trace ie. It's not completely mixed with the lye solution
- You want to prevent your soap from heating up (gel phase) after pouring into the molds by placing in the freezer for a few hours.

Steps to follow when making soap with milk

1. Create or/use a recipe with no water discount.
2. Measure out the water amount in milk and place in ice cube trays to freeze.
3. Place in freezer and allow to freeze.
4. When ready to make soap take milk cubes out of freezer and place in heat resistant pitcher.
5. Measure the lye.
6. Slowly add lye and stir constantly, until fully incorporated.
7. Measure all oils, butters, additives and fragrances.
8. Melt butters and combine with oils.
9. Once oils and butters reach a temperature of 110 degrees Fahrenheit, add the lye solution and continue the cold process method normally.

If you follow this method to substitute milk for the water in your recipes you should not have any problems. You can also look forward to creamy soap that gets hard faster and lathers beautifully. Just be sure to keep the temperatures low.

Part 2 - Recipes

All recipes included in this book will make a 2.5 pound batch of soap. You should always get in the habit of running your recipes through a soap calculator as this allows you to check the proportions for the ingredients and lye solution. You can also adjust the weight to go up or down depending on the size of the mold you are using. Also you can adjust your lye strength, superfat value and fragrance ratios based on your needs and wants. Feel free to swap out the essential oils with your favorites or what you have on hand.

If you make a recipe, please share it with me by posting to the facebook page at **facebook.com/livesoapschool**.

A very popular soap calculator can be found online at **soapcalc.net/calc**. If you need help with using the soap calculator, I have a basic walkthrough available at **livesoapschool.com/soapcalc**.

2.1 Simple Soap
Difficulty*

This is a great introductory plant based soap as the ingredients are relatively simple to gather and give you a fabulous starting point to build on your own. This will lather beautifully and leave the skin squeaky clean.

Recipe
Olive Oil 312 grams (11 ounces)
Coconut Oil 218 grams (7.7 ounces)
Castor Oil 51 grams (1.8 ounces)
Soybean Oil 145 grams (5.1 ounces)

Sodium Hydroxide 103 grams (3.6 ounces)
Distilled Water 276 grams (9.7 ounces)

2.2 Baby Soap

Difficulty*
Our baby soap recipe is one that mom and baby will love. It's super sensitive formulation is perfect for the most delicate skin and ideal for its conditioning properties. This recipe avoids the addition of fragrance or colorant to keep it as mild as possible.

Recipe
Olive Oil 254 grams (9 Ounces)
Mango Butter 145 grams (5.1 Ounces)
Palm Kernel Flakes 145 grams (5.1 Ounces)
Avocado Oil 109 grams (3.8 Ounces)
Castor Oil 73 grams (2.6 Ounces)

Sodium Hydroxide 96 grams (3.4 Ounces)
Distilled Water 276 grams (9.7 Ounces)

2.3 Bastille Soap Recipe
Difficulty: *

Bastille soap is a very gentle cleansing soap. With it's high percentage of olive oil and the addition of coconut oil in the recipe you can expect a moisturizing soap that lathers beautifully. This fragrance-free and color-free recipe is perfect for gentler skin of babies or those with sensitive skin. Note that due to the high percentage of olive oil, you may need to wait an additional 48 hours before unmolding the soap.

Recipe
Olive Oil 472 grams (16.6 ounces)
Coconut Oil 218 grams (7.7 ounces)
Castor Oil 36 grams (1.3 ounces)
Sodium Hydroxide: 103 grams (3.6 ounces)
Distilled Water: 276 grams (9.7 ounces)

2.4 Calming Conditioning Bar
Difficulty: *

Perfect for mature skin. This recipe is full of vitamin rich ingredients and the inclusion of shea butter ensures that moisture remains in the final bar and ultimately on your skin.

Recipe
Rice Bran Oil 327 grams (9.7 ounces)
Babassu Oil 145 grams (5.1 ounces)
Castor Oil 58 grams (2 ounces)
Shea Butter 123 grams (4.3 ounces)
Coconut Oil 73 grams (2.6 ounces)
Sodium Hydroxide: 100 grams (3.5 ounces)
Distilled Water: 276 grams (9.7 ounces)
Lavender Essential Oil 1.6 ounces

2.5 Healing Wonder Recipe
Difficulty: *
A perfect recipe for problematic skin. With the addition of Neem oil, avocado oil and tea tree essential oil this soap earns it's name as the healing wonder that will leave the skin conditioned naturally. This may take a little longer to unmold due to the high amount of soft oils, allow it to sit in the mold for up to 72 hours.

Recipe
Olive Oil 269 Grams (9.5 Ounces)
Coconut Oil 203 Grams (7.17 Ounces)
Avocado Oil 174 Grams (6.1 Ounces)
Castor Oil 36 Grams (1.3 Ounces)
Mango Butter 29 Grams (1.02 Ounces)
Neem Oil 15 Grams (0.5 Ounces)
Tea Tree Essential Oil 1 ounce
Sodium Hydroxide: 102 Grams (3.6 Ounces)
Distilled Water: 261 Grams (9.2 Ounces)

2.6 Lemongrass
Difficulty: *
Lemongrass is anti-bacterial, anti-microbial and a fungicidal with a very pleasant aroma if you love a citrus smell with an earthy undertone. This recipe is a wonderful soap to make a pleasant bar that packs a natural stimulating experience to the senses.

Recipe:
Cocoa Butter 109 grams (3.8 Ounces)
Coconut Oil 218 grams (7.7 Ounces)
Castor Oil 87 grams (3 Ounces)
Almond Oil 29 grams (1 Ounce)
Olive Oil 283 grams (10 Ounces)
Lemongrass Essential Oil 1 Ounce
Sodium Hydroxide 101 grams (3.6 Ounces)
Distilled Water 276 grams (9.7 Ounces)

2.7 Avocado Soap

Difficulty: ***

Avocados aren't only great for the diet, they are fantastic for the skin. With it's ability to deeply penetrate the skin this is a perfect recipe for dry/chapped skin. The double punch of pureed avocado and avocado oil in this recipe is both conditioning and moisturizing.

Special Notes: This recipe incorporates a water discount to account for the additional water content of the pureed avocado.

Recipe:
Rice Bran Oil 140g 36% 261 grams (9.2 ounces)
Avocado Oil 80 g 21% 152 grams (5.4 ounces)
Coconut Oil 120 g 30% 218 grams (1.3 ounces)
Cocoa Butter 30 g 8% 58 grams (2 ounces)
Castor Oil 20 g 5% 36 grams (1.3 ounces)

Sodium Hydroxide: 102 grams
Distilled Water: 261 grams

1 tablespoon of alfalfa powder for colorant
1 ounce of Lemongrass Essential oil
1/2 avocado

Special Note:

To incorporate the avocado you are going to measure and melt all of your oils. You will then add 1/2 an avocado in small chunks to the melted oils. Use your stick blender to puree the avocado until it is smooth with minimal chunks. Once your temperatures of the oils and lye solution are below 90 degrees proceed normally with the soap making process following the cold process method. Once your soap reaches a medium trace add the alfalfa powder and essential oil before pouring the soap batter into the mold.

2.8 Cucumber Pore Perfection

Difficulty: **

Cucumber is known for it's wonderful skin benefits in tightening pores, fading dark spots and reducing puffy eyes but did you know you can use it in soap? This recipe is one of my favorites because it replaces some of the water content with fresh pureed cucumber. Cucumber is naturally full of water along with several nutrients which makes this an ideal bar for problematic skin.

Recipe:
Rice Bran Oil 254 grams (9 Ounces)
Coconut Oil 218 grams (7.7 Ounces)
Shea Butter 73 grams (2.6 Ounces)
Palm Oil 65 grams (2.3 Ounces)
Castor Oil 58 grams (2 Ounces)
Sesame Oil 58 grams (2 Ounces)
Eucalyptus Essential Oil 0.5 ounce
Bergamot Essential Oil 0.5 Ounce

Sodium Hydroxide: 99 grams
Distilled Water: 174 grams
Cucumber Puree: 80 grams

Special Note:
For this recipe you will need one or two cucumbers. Peel the cucumbers and use a food processor or stick blender to puree the cucumber eliminating all chunks. Measure out 80 grams of the fresh puree. You will use this puree with your distilled water to make your lye solution. Combine the cucumber puree with the distilled water. Pour the sodium hydroxide into the distilled water/puree mix and stir well. Once completely stirred continue with the cold process method as normal.

2.9 Egyptian Milk Soap
Difficulty ***

Cleopatra was not only a ruler but was also known for taking luxurious milk baths to preserve a skin. This recipe replaces the water for a blend of coconut milk and almond milk to create a luxuriously creamy and decadent batch of soap.

Recipe:
Kokum Butter 109 grams (3.8 Ounces)
Babassu Oil 145 grams (5.1 Ounces)
Castor Oil 58 grams (2 Ounces)
Avocado Oil 73 grams (2.6 Ounces)
Olive Oil 254 grams (8.9 Ounces)
Shea Butter 87 grams (3 Ounces)
Lavender Essential Oil 0.5 Ounces
Peppermint 0.5 Ounces
Sodium Hydroxide: 93 grams (3.3 Ounces)
Almond Milk - 138 grams (4.9 Ounces)
Coconut Milk - 138 grams (4.9 Ounces)

Special Note:
You will be replacing all of the water content in the lye solution with the almond and coconut milk. If you were to add the lye directly to the liquid milk it would caramelize due to the sugar content in the milk. To avoid this, measure the milk the day before and freeze it in ice cube trays. To make the lye solution, place the milk ice cubes in a pitcher and slowly add the lye to the cubes. Once all lye has been incorporated, stir well to ensure it is blended completely. Continue the soap making process as normal.

Once you have poured the soap into the mold, place the mold in the freezer for about 3 hours to prevent it from heating up. Remove from the freezer and allow it to sit in the mold for an additional 24 hours. After 24 hours you can remove it from the mold, cut into bars and allow it to cure for 5 weeks before using.

2.10 Dead Sea Facial Bar
Difficulty: *

This recipe will create a fantastic lather that naturally cleanses the skin. By incorporating French Green Clay it gently detoxifies the skin while moisturizing. This is a great recipe to try for problematic skin or as a weekly skin ritual for a deep cleanse.

Recipe:
Rice Bran Oil 399 grams (14 Ounces)
Coconut Oil 218 grams (7.7 Ounces)
Castor Oil 36 grams (1.3 Ounces)
Mango Butter 73 grams (2.6 Ounces)
French Green Clay 2 Tablespoons
Tea Tree Essential Oil 1 Ounce

Sodium Hydroxide 101 grams (3.6 Ounces)
Distilled Water 276 grams (9.7 Ounces)

Special Note: To incorporate the French clay, mix your lye and oils like you normally would. Once the soap gets to a thin pudding consistency add your clay and essential oils and blend well. Once completely blended, pour into the mold and allow to set up for 24 hours.

2.11 Soothing Skin Soap

Difficulty: **

Colloidal oats are an excellent addition for itchy irritated skin. Oats are known for their ability to soothe the skin and reduce the urge to scratch. Oatmeal will moisturize and provide a gentle cleanse and help to relieve skin irritations. Fine ground oats can be added within the soap batter and larger oats can be added to the top of the bar for exfoliation and decoration.

Recipe
Almond Oil 87grams (3 Ounces)
Shea Butter 87 grams (3 Ounces)
Coconut Oil 225 grams (7.9 Ounces)
Sunflower Oil 145 grams (5.1 Ounces)
Palm Oil 181 grams (6.4 Ounces)
Ylang Ylang Essential Oil (0.5 Ounces)
Blood Orange Essential Oil (0.5 Ounces)
2 tablespoons of finely ground oatmeal
1/2 cup of Oatmeal

Distilled Water 275 grams (9.7 Ounces)
Sodium Hydroxide 103 grams (3.6 Ounces)

Special Notes:

For this recipe you will need a coffee grinder or food processor to grind 2 tablespoons of the oats into a fine powder. Set aside 1/2 cup of oats to use as decoration on top of the bars once the soap batter is poured into the mold.

2.12 Cooling Cucumber and Aloe Vera Soap

Difficulty: **

Aloe Vera is great for regenerating the skin while also softening and hydrating. This makes it a great ingredient to incorporate for a cleansing and refreshing batch of handmade soap. For this recipe you will be incorporating chilled fresh aloe vera gel along with pureed cucumber for its soothing relief.

Recipe:
Olive Oil 145 grams (5.1 Ounces)
Castor Oil 73 grams (2.6 Ounces)
Coconut Oil 145 grams (5.1 Ounces)
Mango Butter 109 grams (3.8 Ounces)
Palm Oil 181 grams (6.4 Ounces)
Cocoa Butter 73 grams (2.6 Ounces)
Rosemary Essential Oil 0.5 Ounces
Spearmint Essential Oil 0.5 Ounces

Sodium Hydroxide 100 grams (3.5 Ounces)
Aloe Vera Gel and Cucumber Puree 276 grams (9.7 Ounces)

Special Notes:
To prepare for this recipe you will need 2 aloe vera leafs and 2 cucumbers for a total weight of 276 grams. Depending on the size of your aloe vera leaf and cucumber this may require more or less. Extract the aloe vera gel from the plant and peel the cucumbers. Once peeled blend and puree well using a stick blender or magic bullet. Weigh it to ensure you have 276 grams. If it is a little under you can replace missing weight with distilled water. Chill in the refrigerator for about 3 hours. When you are ready to make soap you will use the pureed mixture of aloe vera gel and cucumber as your water portion in the lye solution.

2.13 One Oil Wonder
Difficulty: *

This recipe will create a very white bar of soap that is very cleansing and moisturizing with an incredible lather. It's all coconut oil which could be drying but we adjust that outcome by adding additional oil in the recipe to make the perfect balanced bar. Try this recipe for a single ingredient soap or as a starter for trying your hand at incorporating color into your recipes. Feel free to add 1 ounce of your favorite essential oil or fragrance oils to truly make it your own.

Recipe:
Coconut Oil 726 grams (25.6 Ounces)

Distilled Water: 276 grams (9.7 Ounces)
Sodium Hydroxide 113 grams (4 Ounces)

2.14 Palm Free Recipe
Due to the controversy with sustainable palm oil, you may decide to eliminate palm oil from your ingredients completely. This recipe will make a hard bar that is cleansing and lathers beautifully without the use of palm oil.

Recipe:
Cocoa Butter 73 grams (2.6 Ounces)
Coconut Oil 254 grams (8.9 Ounces)
Olive Oil 218 grams (7.7 Ounces)
Castor Oil 36 grams (1.3 Ounces)
Sunflower Oil 145 grams (5.1 Ounces)

Distilled Water 276 grams (9.7 Ounces)
Sodium Hydroxide 104 grams (3.7 Ounces)

2.15 Activated Charcoal Cleansing Bar
Difficulty: *

Activated charcoal has become a very popular ingredient for skincare and for good reason! It's ability to naturally cleanse the skin and clean pores makes it an excellent addition for both color and the qualities it lends the final batch of soap. Be careful this fine powder gets everywhere when airborne, use caution and consider using disposable cups or stainless steel to measure activated charcoal.

Recipe
Coconut Oil 165 grams (5.8 Ounces)
Olive Oil 177 grams (6.2 Ounces)
Castor Oil 47 grams (1.7 Ounces)
Palm Oil 112 grams (3.9 Ounces)
Kokum Butter 88 grams (3.1 Ounces)
Activated Charcoal 2 Tablespoons

Sodium Hydroxide: 83 grams (2.9 Ounces)
Distilled Water: 224 grams (7.9 Ounces)

Special Notes: To incorporate activated charcoal in your recipe, follow all cold processing steps as normal. Once your soap batter is at a light trace you can add the activated charcoal and blend until it's smooth before pouring it into the mold. You can also separate half of the batter to leave uncolored and only incorporate the activated charcoal in one portion before pouring into the mold.

2.16 Sea Salt Bar
Difficulty: **

The Sea Salt Spa Escape recipe will give you a spa like bar that is hard and exfoliating due to the salt content. Do not use dead sea salt in this recipe as it will cause a weeping effect in your soap. Salt is also known to be a lather killer so we combat this by increasing our coconut oil and superfatting at 20% to prevent the drying effect that could be caused by using too much coconut oil in the recipe.

Recipe:
Coconut Oil: 471 grams (16.6 Ounces)
Castor Oil: 88 grams (3.1 Ounces)
Shea Butter: 29 grams (1 Ounces)
Pink Himalayan Sea Salt: 14 Ounces
Rosemary Essential Oil: 0.5 Ounces
Lemon Essential Oil: 0.5 Ounces

Sodium Hydroxide: 81 grams (2.9 Ounces)
Distilled Water: 224 grams (7.9 Ounces)

Special Notes:
Once your soap batter reaches a light trace, add the essential oils and Himalayan Sea Salt to the batter and pour into the mold. It should Harden within 4 to 6 hours, some ready to take it out quickly. Consider using individual cavity molds to help release the soap quicker. Once taken out of the molds allow the soap to cure normally.

Part 3 - Creating your own Vegan Soap Recipes

You can and should create your own recipes. Once you are comfortable with the soap making process you may find that the recipes you use aren't quite giving you what you desire. Or you may want to substitute one oil for another.

By creating your own recipes you meticulously decide on the type of soap you are formulating along with all of the ingredients you will use. This section highlights the most popular plant based ingredients and the qualities they will offer your soap.

3.0 The DNA of Oils and Butters

Will you make an exfoliating bar? A bar specifically crafted for oily skin? Dry skin? Mature skin? Acne prone skin? The truth is with a little knowledge of the oil's DNA you can formulate anything you want… within reason. I'm not promising the miracle cure for acne but you can get pretty darn close. It all begins with the Fatty Acid Profile, I often refer to this as the DNA of oils and butters. Let's start by comparing the DNA of two of the most popular oils used in soap making, Coconut oil and Olive oil.

Fatty Acids	Coconut Oil	Olive Oil
Lauric (cleansing)	48	0
Myristic (fluffy lather)	19	0
Palmitic (cleansing)	9	14
Stearic (hardness)	3	3
Ricinoleic (creamy)	0	0
Oleic (conditioning)	8	69
Linoleic (moisture)	2	12
Linolenic (conditioning)	0	1

Notice that they actually contain a combination of several fatty acids in each oil. No oil has just one fatty acid. It's the concentration of different fatty acids at different levels that makes each oil unique. In selecting oils for your recipes you are attempting to achieve the optimal balance for the qualities you want in the batches you create. You will need to consider trade offs for increasing one oil over another. You will need to consider recommended usage rates to avoid creating a bar that is overly drying to the skin, or one that will not lather or bars that will be too soft. These are all considered to be undesirable characteristics of handcrafted soap. Your understanding of what each fatty acid contributes to a batch of soap will help you to create balanced recipes.

The true power of any oil or butter you select for your creations comes from its fatty acid profile. Each oil has a unique make up or combination of fatty acids. The fatty acid profile is what determines if you will have a fluffy lather, creamy lather, emollient soap, cleansing soap or moisturizing soap. There are eight fatty acids we must come to understand as soap makers as these are what define the qualities of the bars we will make. Make no mistake when someone mentions the benefits of coconut oil or Kokum butter the name may sound intriguing but it's true wonder comes from the fatty acids that make up the oil or butter. Listed below are 8 fatty acids that we consider for the oils and butters we choose for handmade soap recipes.

1. Lauric Acid
2. Linoleic Acid
3. Linolenic Acid
4. Myristic Acid
5. Oleic Acid
6. Palmitic Acid
7. Ricinoleic Acid
8. Stearic Acid

Lauric Acid - When you think of Lauric think of cleansing. I often remember this by thinking of Laundry detergent. Simply because Lauric and laundry sound similar in my mind. Lauric acid contributes cleansing properties to soap. So much so that too much Lauric acid in a bar of soap can be stripping to the skin. Lauric acid also contributes to hardness of the bar along with fluffy lather. Armed with this information, if you know that you are attempting to formulate a bar of soap for oily skin you may look for a higher percentage of Lauric acid in your formulation. If you were attempting to craft a shampoo bar that can be used to remove excess product buildup from the hair. A high dose of lauric acid may be just what you need. This can also be used for troubleshooting or balancing recipes. If you notice that you bar isn't producing much lather, did you have enough ingredients containing Lauric acid which would contribute to the lather?

Ingredients with high percentage of Lauric Acid:
- Coconut Oil
- Palm Kernel Oil
- Palm Oil
- Babassu Oil

Linoleic: Great for moisture and conditioning qualities it lends to soap. Linoleic acid can also add a silky feel to the bar. The one downside to this is many of the ingredients that have high percentages of linoleic acid also have a shorter shelf life. What this means is if you incorporate a high percentage of oils with linoleic acid you are more likely to see orange spots appearing in your bars as the oils have gone rancid. This is not to say that you should avoid this fatty acid, in fact it may be difficult to avoid it all together instead remain mindful when you are creating your recipes and limit the percentage of these ingredients as you are creating balanced recipes.

Ingredients with high percentage of Linoleic Acid:
- Sunflower Oil
- Safflower Oil
- Grapeseed Oil

Linolenic Acid: If you are looking for conditioning, linolenic acid will contribute this quality to your soap. Similar to linoleic the oils that have the highest percentage of this fatty acid have shorter shelf lives, so it must be used sparingly in soap recipes. I often use this for it's luxurious feel it contributes as well. This fatty acid also contributes to a mild bar of soap so its perfect for babies and sensitive skin formulations.

Ingredients with high percentage of Linoleic Acid:

- **Flaxseed Oil**

Myristic Acid: When you need to add fluffy lather and cleansing qualities to your bar look for oils with Myristic acid. This fatty acid also imparts hardness to your bar and when formulated correctly with other fatty acids the outcome is incredible. Most oils that have high percentages of myristic acid are also fairly easy to get with a stable shelf life which makes it a nice addition to your soap recipes. Similar to Lauric acid you want to be careful not to overdo it with this particular fatty acid as it can become drying.

Ingredients with high percentage of Myristic Acid:
- Nutmeg Butter
- Coconut Oil
- Palm Oil

Oleic Acid: If you want to make a gentle bar of soap, oleic acid is where you should begin. This fatty acid contributes conditioning and moisturizing properties to the finished bar. However too much oleic acid will lead to a very soft bar or a bar that takes forever to cure like a Castile bar of soap (100% olive oil). Oleic acid also tends to slow down the soap making process so this helps when you need time to work with recipes for intricate designs and swirls.

Ingredients with high percentage of Oleic Acid
- **Olive Oil**
- **Canola Oil**
- **Sunflower Oil**
- **Sweet Almond Oil**

Palmitic Acid: You may want to make a creamy lather and this is where palmitic acid will shine. If you need to stabilize the lather palmitic acid will help. While this fatty acid contributes hardness and longevity to a batch of soap it also makes for a very creamy lather. Think of this for your facial soap as many people enjoy a creamy feel to products applied to the face.

Ingredients with high percentage of Palm Oil
Palm Oil
Cocoa Butter
Avocado Butter

Ricinoleic Acid: This fatty acid is a wonder to the handcrafted soap maker. It is only found in Castor oil and is a work horse in natural soap recipes. It contributes to the hardness of soap, stabilizes the lather while creating large bubbles AND adds moisture. Too much of this fatty acid can make for a sticky bar but when used appropriately the results are optimal for many recipes.

Ingredient with high percentage of Ricinoleic Acid:
- **Castor Oil**

Stearic Acid: This is where butters and waxes shine for soap makers. Stearic Acid contributes to hardness of soap with a creamy lather. If you are looking to create a mens shaving soap or need something to harden an otherwise soft batch of soap, stearic acid may do the trick for you.

Ingredients with high percentage of Stearic Acid:
- Mango Butter
- Shea Butter
- Kokum Butter
- Cocoa Butter

Your understanding of Fatty Acids and how they contribute to a recipe will also help you when it comes to substituting oils and butters in recipes. Aside from their SAP values which we will discuss shortly, the fatty acid profile will help you decide that cocoa butter may be an acceptable substitute for shea butter but then again it could throw your entire recipe off depending on the other ingredients in the recipe.

What I want you to take from this information is an understanding of what each fatty acid contributes to a soap recipe and use this to start thinking of the qualities you want in your soap. Remember every soap maker is different and every batch can be different if you so choose.

One of the most common questions I hear is, "Can I substitute palm oil for olive oil or shea butter for almond oil". Once you understand these properties and how they impact a batch of soap you will know the answer to these questions is Yes, No or Maybe depending on the oil and how you reformulate the recipe.

Saturated Fat & Unsaturated Fat

We can't end our discussion on fatty acids without a brief discussion of saturated fats and unsaturated fats. For our purposes in soap making the overall balance between saturated fats and unsaturated fats will contribute positively or negatively to our final batch of soap. I don't want you to be overly concerned with saturated fats and unsaturated fats but this information may come in handy when attempting to troubleshoot problematic recipes or when you are trying to balance a recipe.

Saturated Fats are typically solid at room temperature and unsaturated fats are liquid at room temperature. Typically oils that are high in stearic or palmitic acid are saturated fats and they contribute to a hard bar of soap. Conversely, unsaturated fats are liquid at room temperature and can contribute to a softer bar of soap.

Unsaturated fats also contribute the highest percentage of skin nourishing qualities like moisture and condition so they typically prove to be beneficial in recipes. Unsaturated fats also have shorter shelf lives and too high of a percentage of unsaturated fats in recipes can lead to your soap going rancid.

Balance is key and unfortunately there is no hard and fast rule as to what the right balance should be. As you begin to create your own recipes start with a 60:40 ratio of 60% saturated and 40% unsaturated and work your way to an ideal balance based on what you like in the final outcome.

3.1 Saponification, SAP value and SuperFat

This is a very basic overview of soaping terms that are important in understanding soap making particularly relative to ingredients and recipes.

Saponification is the process of making soap. Soap is made from fats, oils and alkalis that result in a sodium salt that has cleansing properties in water. In order for this process to occur the fats and oils must be converted with an alkali. To determine how much of the alkali is needed we must know the oil's SAP value. SAP value represents the number of milligrams of potassium hydroxide or sodium hydroxide required to completely saponify one gram of fat or oil. For cold process soap making we use sodium hydroxide.

SAP value stands for the Saponification value. Every oil and butter in soap recipes has a unique SAP value. Put another way, understanding the SAP value helps us to formulate recipes with the precise amount of lye (sodium hydroxide or potassium hydroxide) needed to cause the reaction. This makes SAP value a pretty big deal, but not something to get over concerned with.

There are several online soap and lye calculators that will do the math for you but it's important for you to have a basic understanding of what the SAP value is and why it matters. Simply enter soap calculator or lye calculator in your favorite search engine and try a few. I offer hands on recipe formulation and soap calculation training at **https:// class.livesoapschool.com**. If you need additional support or

recipe consultations I would love to help you.

If we simply go with the exact amount of lye needed to cause the soap reaction that's a very basic and sometimes unforgiving soap recipe. For this reason Superfatting is done. Superfatting is a method soap makers use to incorporate more oil or butter than required in a recipe so that the qualities remain in the final bar while also offering some wiggle room in the soap pot. Most soap makers stay within the range of 3-10% for superfatting but this is a matter of personal preference along with considerations for the oils in the recipe.

Saponification is the term used to describe the soap making process. In order to complete this process we need to know and leverage the SAP value to ensure we don't over do it with the lye.

3.2 Vegan Ingredient Profiles

Every oil and butter is made up of various fatty acid profiles that lend a different outcome to your final batch of soap. Some are high in conditioning while others are high in cleansing or moisturizing qualities. Vegan soap can be very enriching to the skin as it is constituted of the best qualities that nature intended.

Your understanding of these ingredients will help you create your own unique signature recipes. Take some time to review each of the following plant based ingredients and refer back to it once you are ready to start making your own combinations.

Each Ingredient lists:
- Ingredient Name - Common name used to refer to the ingredient
- INCI Name - International Nomenclature of Cosmetic Ingredients
- Shelf Life - How long the ingredient lasts before going rancid
- Saponification Value - the amount of sodium hydroxide or potassium hydroxide need to saponify 1 gram of this particular ingredient
- Characteristics of the ingredient - this lists some of the skin benefits of the ingredients.
- Fatty Acid Profile - qualities that it imparts in the final batch of soap
- Recommended Usage rates - percentages to incorporate in your own recipe

All of the recommendations are only meant to be starting guidelines. As you progress in soap making your experience and preferences will guide you to the perfect balance for your desired soap qualities.

Look at each of the ingredients and determine which qualities you desire in your final batch, once you identify these oils this should be the base of your ingredient shopping list. Here's a word to the wise start with 3 staple ingredients of olive oil, coconut oil and palm oil. Once you are confident with making your own recipes and the soap making process you can build on additional ingredients as you grow in your recipe creations.

3.3 Almond Oil

INCI NAME: Prunus Dulcis
Shelf Life: 1 year
Sodium Hydroxide (NAOH) SAP Value: 0.1367
Potassium Hydroxide (KOH) SAP Value: 0.1925
Characteristics: Typically contributes little to lather but an extremely conditioning and emollient ingredient. Almond oil is a great addition to any recipe targeted at moisturizing and softening the skin. Can be used as a substitute for avocado oil.
Fatty Acid Profile: Hardness x |Cleansing | Conditioning x | Bubbly Lather| Creamy Lather x
Usage Recommendations: Up to 10%

3.4 Avocado Oil

INCI NAME: Persea Gratissima
Shelf Life: 1 Year
Sodium Hydroxide (NAOH) SAP Value: 0.1337
Potassium Hydroxide (KOH) SAP Value: 0.1883
Characteristics: Avocado oil offers mild cleansing to your recipe and mid-size lathering qualities. Due to its high make up of vitamins and minerals consider adding to facial soap recipes. Avocado oil easily penetrates the skin, it is naturally moisturizing and soothing making it a fantastic ingredient for problematic skin. This oil has a high percentage of unsaponifables so many of the qualities will remain in the final batch of soap. Can be used as a substitute for sweet almond oil.
Fatty Acid Profile: Hardness x |Cleansing | Conditioning x | Bubbly Lather| Creamy Lather x
Usage Recommendations: Up to 20%

3.5 Babassu Oil

INCI NAME: Orbignya Oleifera
Shelf Life: 2 years
Sodium Hydroxide (NAOH) SAP Value: 0.1749
Potassium Hydroxide (KOH) SAP Value: 0.2463
Characteristics: A great substitute for coconut oil and palm oil as the fatty acid profiles are similar. Babassu oil is gentler for sensitive skin and will contribute fluffy lather and cleansing properties in your soap recipes.
Fatty Acid Profile: Hardness x | Cleansing x | Conditioning | Bubbly Lather x| Creamy Lather
Usage Recommendations: Up to 30%

3.6 Canola Oil

INCI NAME: Canola Oil
Shelf Life: 1 year
Sodium Hydroxide (NAOH) SAP Value: 0.1328
Potassium Hydroxide (KOH) SAP Value: 0.1870
Characteristics: Contributes to a stable lather and is often used to replace a portion of rice bran oil or olive oil due to its fatty acid profile. Canola oil contains anti-oxidants and vitamins and you can expect an extremely conditioning and moisturizing bar with a creamy lather.
Fatty Acid Profile: Hardness |Cleansing | Conditioning x | Bubbly Lather| Creamy Lather x
Usage Recommendations: Up to 30%

3.7 Castor Oil

INCI NAME: Ricinus Communis (Castor) Seed oil
Shelf Life: 2 years
Sodium Hydroxide (NAOH) SAP Value: 0.1286
Potassium Hydroxide (KOH) SAP Value: 0.1811
Characteristics: Contributes to a rich and creamy stable lather in your soap recipes when used in combination with coconut oil. A little goes a long way with this ingredient you will not need more than 8% in any recipe but can go as high as 10%. Beware, castor oil can speed up your trace so if you want to do intricate swirls, keep this ingredient to a minimum in your recipes.
Fatty Acid Profile: Hardness |Cleansing | Conditioning x | Bubbly Lather| Creamy Lather x
Usage Recommendations: Up to 10%

3.8 Cocoa Butter

INCI NAME: Theobroma Cacao (Cococoa) Seed Butter
Shelf Life: 2 years
Sodium Hydroxide (NAOH) SAP Value: 0.1378
Potassium Hydroxide (KOH) SAP Value: 0.1941
Characteristics: Contributes to harder bar of soap as well as moisture on the skin. Cocoa butter isn't easily absorbed by the skin so it is best to incorporate with other ingredients like rice bran oil or olive oil. Try not to exceed 15% of cocoa butter in your total recipe to avoid getting a brittle bar.
Fatty Acid Profile: Hardness x |Cleansing | Conditioning x | Bubbly Lather| Creamy Lather x
Usage Recommendations: Up to 15%

3.9 Coconut Oil

INCI NAME: Cocos Nucifera (Coconut) Oil
Shelf Life: 2 years
Sodium Hydroxide (NAOH) SAP Value: 0.1910
Potassium Hydroxide (KOH) SAP Value: 0.2690
Characteristics: To many soap makers coconut oil is one of the holy grail oils of soap making. Due to it's versatile fatty acid profile. You can expect cleansing, moisture and lots of lather from this ingredient. You can also achieve a whiter bar of soap with coconut oil.
Fatty Acid Profile: Hardness x |Cleansing x | Conditioning | Bubbly Lather x | Creamy Lather
Usage Recommendations: Up to 30%

3.10 Grapeseed Oil

INCI NAME: Vitis Vinifera (Grape) Seed Oil
Shelf Life: 1 year
Sodium Hydroxide (NAOH) SAP Value: 0.1321
Potassium Hydroxide (KOH) SAP Value: 0.1861
Characteristics: Very popular for its ability to penetrate the skin however it should be used in moderation due to the short shelf life, it can go rancid in as little as 6 months. If you need to up the conditioning qualities in your recipe, consider adding grapeseed oil.
Fatty Acid Profile: Hardness |Cleansing | Conditioning x | Bubbly Lather| Creamy Lather
Usage Recommendations: Up to 15%

3.11 Jojoba Oil

INCI NAME: Simmondsia Chinensis (Jojoba) Seed Oil
Shelf Life: 2 years
Sodium Hydroxide (NAOH) SAP Value: 0.0695
Potassium Hydroxide (KOH) SAP Value: 0.0979
Characteristics: This is considered a luxury oil and comes at a premium however it will regulate the lather and has incredible moisturizing properties. Jojoba oil easily penetrates the skin which makes it a great ingredient for a conditioning bar of soap. It also has a longer shelf life than grapeseed oil so can be used in its place in recipes.
Fatty Acid Profile: Hardness |Cleansing | Conditioning x | Bubbly Lather| Creamy Lather
Usage Recommendations: Up to 10%

3.12 Kokum Butter

INCI NAME: Garcinia Indica (Kokum) Butter
Shelf Life: 2 years
Sodium Hydroxide (NAOH) SAP Value: 0.1350
Potassium Hydroxide (KOH) SAP Value: 0.1900
Characteristics: Kokum butter does not clog pores which makes it a great ingredient for sensitive skin recipes. Due to the fatty acid profile it will help to moisturize, condition and soften the skin. It makes a great substitute for cocoa butter in your recipes. Great ingredient for damaged skin.
Fatty Acid Profile: Hardness x |Cleansing | Conditioning x | Bubbly Lather x | Creamy Lather
Usage Recommendations: Up to 10%

3.13 Mango Butter

INCI NAME: Mangifera Indica (Mango) Seed Butter
Shelf Life: 2 years
Sodium Hydroxide (NAOH) SAP Value: 0.1360
Potassium Hydroxide (KOH) SAP Value: 0.1910
Characteristics: Also known as a healing butter with emollient properties which makes it very conditioning for the skin. You can expect a rich creamy lather with mango butter.
Fatty Acid Profile: Hardness x |Cleansing | Conditioning x | Bubbly Lather| Creamy Lather x
Usage Recommendations: Up to 20%

3.14 Neem Oil

INCI NAME: Melia Azadirachta Seed Oil
Shelf Life: 2 years
Sodium Hydroxide (NAOH) SAP Value: 0.1372
Potassium Hydroxide (KOH) SAP Value: 0.1932
Characteristics: Watch out, Neem oil has a very distinctive and strong odor but it's benefits highly outweigh the smell which can be masked with essential oils and fragrance oils. Neem oil is known for it's healing qualities and is known as a wonder oil in soap making.
Fatty Acid Profile: Hardness x |Cleansing | Conditioning x | Bubbly Lather| Creamy Lather x
Usage Recommendations: Up to 5%

3.15 Olive Oil

INCI NAME: Olea Europaea
Shelf Life: 2 years
Sodium Hydroxide (NAOH) SAP Value: 0.1353
Potassium Hydroxide (KOH) SAP Value: 0.1906
Characteristics: Another staple and holy grail oil for most soap makers is Olive Oil. With it's hypoallergenic properties it is great for all skin types and provides moisture that easily penetrates the skin. Olive oils very mild on the skin and gentle on the most sensitive of skin. It can be substituted for canola oil or rice bran oil in your recipes.
Fatty Acid Profile: Hardness |Cleansing | Conditioning x | Bubbly Lather| Creamy Lather x
Usage Recommendations: Can be used up to 100% if making Castile soap, however you will have a very long curing period of up to 1 year. Best if used at a maximum of 50% in combination with hard oils to avoid a soft soap.

3.16 Palm Oil

INCI NAME: Elaeis Guineensis (Palm) Oil
Shelf Life: 1 year
Sodium Hydroxide (NAOH) SAP Value: 0.1420
Potassium Hydroxide (KOH) SAP Value: 0.2000
Characteristics: If you are struggling with hardness in your soap, palm oil is a great addition to up the hardness quality. Palm oil is packed with vitamins and minerals that are great for the skin and contributes to a creamy lather. There is a palm oil controversy happening now which questions the sustainability of palm oil sourcing. If you would prefer to stay away from palm oil you can substitute with Babassu oil or coconut oil.
Fatty Acid Profile: Hardness x |Cleansing x | Conditioning x | Bubbly Lather| Creamy Lather x
Usage Recommendations: Up to 30%

3.17 Palm Kernel Oil

INCI NAME: Elaseis Guineensis
Shelf Life: 1 year
Sodium Hydroxide (NAOH) SAP Value: 0.1361
Potassium Hydroxide (KOH) SAP Value: 0.2503
Characteristics: Palm kernel oil creates a white hard bar of soap that is full of lather. Because it generally creates a white bar this is a great base for coloring natural soap. Palm Kernel oil is loaded with antioxidants, vitamins which makes it perfect for nourishing the skin. This oil is not to be confused with palm oil as it has a very different fatty acid profile, SAP value and properties it will lend the final bar of soap. This can be substituted for coconut oil and babassu oil in recipes.
Fatty Acid Profile: Hardness x |Cleansing x | Conditioning | Bubbly Lather x| Creamy Lather
Usage Recommendations: Up to 30%

3.18 Rice Bran Oil

INCI NAME: Oryza Sativa
Shelf Life: 2 years
Sodium Hydroxide (NAOH) SAP Value: 0.1284
Potassium Hydroxide (KOH) SAP Value: 0.1808
Characteristics: Rice Bran oil is considered to be hypoallergenic and therefore won't clog pores. It consists of a healthy dose of vitamin E and is highly moisturizing. This is a great addition for mature and sensitive skin as it's not drying or stripping. This can be substituted for olive oil in recipes.
Fatty Acid Profile: Hardness |Cleansing | Conditioning x | Bubbly Lather| Creamy Lather x
Usage Recommendations: Up to 30%

3.19 Sesame Seed Oil

INCI NAME: Carthamus Tinctorius
Shelf Life: 1 year
Sodium Hydroxide (NAOH) SAP Value: 0.1340
Potassium Hydroxide (KOH) SAP Value: 0.1880
Characteristics: Sesame seed oil contributes a silky luxurious feel along with a conditioning quality to your recipe. It is also great for skin ailments and can be used to superfat soap so the nourishing qualities remain in the final bar of soap.
Fatty Acid Profile: Hardness |Cleansing | Conditioning x | Bubbly Lather| Creamy Lather x
Usage Recommendations: Up to 10%

3.20 Shea Butter

INCI NAME: Butyrosepermum parkii
Shelf Life: 2 years
Sodium Hydroxide (NAOH) SAP Value: 0.1296
Potassium Hydroxide (KOH) SAP Value: 0.1825
Characteristics: Shea Butter is another one of those ingredients that soap makers love. It has a very high percentage of unsaponifiables which means many of it's benefits remain in the final bar once it goes through saponification. This is a fantastic addition if you are attempting to create a moisturizing recipe that nourishes the skin with a silky feel to the soap.
Fatty Acid Profile: Hardness x |Cleansing | Conditioning x | Bubbly Lather| Creamy Lather x **Usage Recommendations:** Up to 20%

3.21 Sunflower Oil

INCI NAME: Helianthus Annuus
Shelf Life: 6 Months
Sodium Hydroxide (NAOH) SAP Value: 0.1358
Potassium Hydroxide (KOH) SAP Value: 0.1913
Characteristics: Sunflower oil has a high Vitamin E content which makes it an ideal addition to your soap recipes. It also adds conditioning and harness to your soap.
Fatty Acid Profile: Hardness |Cleansing | Conditioning x | Bubbly Lather| Creamy Lather x
Usage Recommendations: Up to 20%

SOAPERS NOTES:

Think about the type of soap you would like to create. Now take a look at each of the oils and butters. Which ones will you use in your upcoming recipes and why?

4.0 A Makers Tale

You have made it to the end of the cookbook and I want to share my start and most important lesson with you. I stumbled across a video online demonstrating someone doing something with colors and found it completely mesmerizing and I was unable to look away. This lady was making soap. I tried to make sense of the videos but I always felt like there was something missing. Something they just weren't telling me, some piece of the puzzle that was being left out. In hindsight the only missing piece was me trying it for myself.

Soap making was a way to escape reality. I was truly seeking work life balance and what I found was nothing short of magical. Not only did it give me a creative outlet, it allowed me to connect with viewers and readers all over the world while starting and growing a business. It didn't start out this way but magic happens when you follow your heart and allow your mind to get out of the way.

I started reading every book I could find while simultaneously stockpiling every oil, butter, mold, fragrance oil and colorant mentioned in the books but I never actually made anything for the first two months. I was afraid of the lye, I was afraid it wouldn't work, I was afraid that it wouldn't be as beautiful as the pictures and videos I had seen. As my family watched all of these supplies and ingredients come into the house they started questioning what in the world I was up to. Then one day I decided it would be cool just to see what would happen. If it didn't work I would call myself the mad scientist. If it worked I would be SoapLadyZ. I guess you know the ending to this story because you are now reading my third book on soap making. Not only did it work out, I was able to recapture my inner artist while creating incredible products for my friends, family and customers from all over the world.

I'm telling you this story because believe it or not you now have EVERYTHING you need but one piece and that piece is you actually picking up your stick blender and committing to the process. The process of discovery which includes getting it right, getting it wrong and learning from every batch. Your success or failure will simply come down to your intent and how you chose to look at your creations. Allow yourself to be an artist flaws and all. That's when you will experience the magic of soap making and beyond.

Share your artistry with me by posting to the Live Soap School page on facebook **facebook.com/livesoapschool** or using the hashtag #LiveSoapSchool on Instagram.

I wish you much success in your journey of discovery.
-SoapLadyZ

4.1 Stay Connected

Loved this book? Leave us a review on Amazon!

Still concerned -- a little overwhelmed? Would you feel better if you had someone to explain a few things first-hand? Would asking questions or sharing the experience with classmates help ease your mind? You can get more information when you follow the links below.

HOW TO STAY CONNECTED

ENROLL IN SOAP SCHOOL AT CLASS.LIVESOAPSCHOOL.COM

Learn to create your own recipes by taking an in-depth course in Live Soap School. Develop your skills as you discover how to make hot process soap, cold process soap, how to use online soap calculators, gain advanced design techniques and more in a supportive hands-on self-paced training.

STAY UP TO DATE ON THE BLOG AT LIVESOAPSCHOOL.COM
Subscribe to the free blog where Zakia blogs regularly and includes current lessons learned, how-to's and broadcast archives.

CONNECT ON SOCIAL MEDIA

FACEBOOK - Join us at **facebook.com/livesoapschool** to watch a soap making live stream broadcast and ask your questions.

TWITTER - Catch Zakia live on her daily live vlog on twitter at **twitter.com/zakiaringgold**

INSTAGRAM - Follow Live Soap School on Instagram for DIY tips, soap inspiration, and behind the scenes tutorials at: **instagram.com/livesoapschool**

4.2 Read My Books for Soap Makers

New Soap Makers Cookbook - Ingredients for Success

Learn key ingredients to get you started while side stepping some of the most common missteps of new soap makers. There are simple "ingredients" to shift your paradigm on your new craft going all the way up to cold process soap making. This is a great place to start or reignite crafting your own handmade soap. You may find you already have most of the ingredients right now, without stepping into a single store.

New Soap Makers Cookbook Making Cold Process Soap From Scratch

This no-nonsense approach cookbook takes the fluff out of cold process soap making so you can proceed with confidence and start making your own soap quickly. Get all of the basics including: soap safety, working with lye, supplies, step by step instructions, easy recipes with simple ingredients and more.

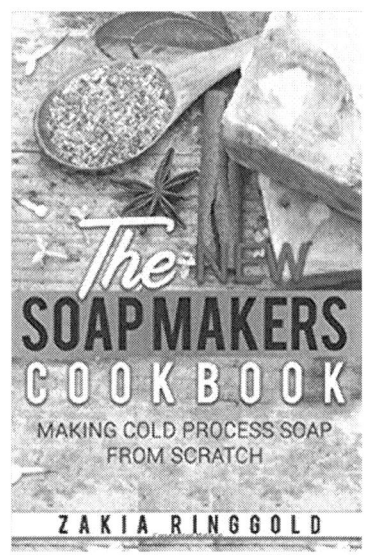

4.3 About the Author

For Zakia Ringgold, magic happens when motherhood collides with life, work and technology. Seeking work/life balance and surrounded by a supportive family, she launched her online soap shop NaturalSoapByZakia.com. She did this with a live stream and a cellphone to the tune of 100 orders in the first week, without leaving her dining room. She realized it was so much more than soap, it was education, self-expression, opportunity, empowerment and most importantly community.

Zakia teaches youth and budding hobbyist turned business owners soap making and digital technology. With over 15 years experience developing training curriculum, Ringgold decided to lean into her passion of soap making and combine it with her skillset to make instructional programs and digital solutions.

Soap Making, live streaming and digital technology with simple instructions are the foundations on which Zakia bases her services. This has placed her in the international space, shipping her product line to 17 countries and counting, while training students globally to do the same at LiveSoapSchool.com.

She is a certified Soap Maker through the Soap Guild and author of The New Soap Makers Cookbook series. Watch Zakia and her family broadcasting live on your favorite social media platform @ZakiaRinggold.

Soap making will be whatever you make it. It can either be a lifetime hobby that you share with your close family and friends or a growing business.

Approach it every day with the same curiosity that got you interested in the first place and you will enjoy it for years to come.

—SoapLadyZ

Made in the USA
Monee, IL
23 August 2020